THE
BOOK OF THE
BARN OWL

Bestselling author Sally Coulthard has spent the past two decades writing about nature, history and craft. Many of her books delve into the traditions of rural life – from artisans to agriculture – the people, plants and creatures who make the countryside tick. She lives on a North Yorkshire smallholding with her family and animals.

First published in the UK in 2022 by Head of Zeus
This paperback edition first published in 2023 by Head of Zeus,
part of Bloomsbury Publishing Plc

9 7 5 3 1 2 4 6 8

A catalogue record for this book is available from
the British Library.

ISBN (PB): 9781803289335
ISBN (E): 9781789544763

Typeset by Francesca Mangiaracina
Illustrations © Vanessa Lubach

Printed and bound in Great Britain by
CPI Group (UK) Ltd, Croydon CR0 4YY

Head of Zeus Ltd
5–8 Hardwick Street
London EC1R 4RG
WWW.HEADOFZEUS.COM

THE
BOOK OF THE
BARN OWL

Sally Coulthard

HEAD
ZEUS

An Apollo Book

For Edward

CONTENTS

Introduction

THE OWL

Downhill I came, hungry, and yet not starved;
Cold, yet had heat within me that was proof
Against the North wind; tired, yet so that rest
Had seemed the sweetest thing under a roof.

Then at the inn I had food, fire, and rest,
Knowing how hungry, cold, and tired was I.
All of the night was quite barred out except
An owl's cry, a most melancholy cry

Shaken out long and clear upon the hill,
No merry note, nor cause of merriment,
But one telling me plain what I escaped
And others could not, that night, as in I went.

And salted was my food, and my repose,
Salted and sobered, too, by the bird's voice
Speaking for all who lay under the stars,
Soldiers and poor, unable to rejoice.

BY EDWARD THOMAS (1878–1917)

When Edward Thomas wrote his poem 'The Owl', he never made it clear which species he imagined, penetrating the darkness with its 'most melancholy cry'. Some have thought of it as the twit-twoo of the tawny, Britain's most common owl, but for me, it could only be one creature – the elusive barn owl. Few birds have such an otherworldly call, a long eerie shriek 'shaken out long and clear upon the hill'. Heard in the depths of midnight, it's enough to send a shiver down the spines of both mice and men.

For most of history, the barn owl was named after its voice, not its home. People in the Middle Ages knew the bird as the 'scritche-owle' or screech-owl, its cry a harbinger of death or disaster. Medieval bestiaries thought the bird an ill omen, a creature who frequented dark caves, cemeteries and tombs. As Shakespeare warned in *A Midsummer Night's Dream*:

> *Now the wasted brands do glow*
> *Whilst the screech-owl, screeching loud,*

Puts the wretch that lies in woe
In remembrance of a shroud.

Even early scientific papers on barn owls couldn't resist dipping into the language of the morgue. Francis Willughby, the seventeenth-century ornithologist who was one of the first to use the term 'barn owl', indulged readers with a lugubrious and detailed description of its face. 'A circle or wreath', he wrote, 'of white, soft, downy feathers encompassed with yellow ones, beginning from the Nosthrils on each side, passed round the Eyes and under the Chin, somewhat resembling a black hood, such as women use to wear: So that the Eyes were sunk in the middle of these feathers, as it were in the bottom of a Pit or Valley.'[1]

With so few people on its side, it's perhaps no wonder the barn owl – for most of its co-existence with humans – had few friends. A series of Tudor Acts of Parliament, aimed specifically at 'Noyfull Fowles and Vermin', put a bounty on wild mammals' and birds' heads – not least the barn owl. Villagers could earn good money when they were paid a penny for 'every six young owls, and a penny for six unbroken eggs'.[2] The barn owls' nocturnal screams and silent flight also made them ripe for superstition; to see one out in the daytime was long considered unlucky, while its plaintive cry warned calamity was surely on its way. Some superstitions were just plain odd – in Wales, its unholy screech signalled the passing of a girl's chastity, while in Yorkshire nothing cleared up whooping cough like a steaming bowl of barn owl broth.[3]

But then something shifted. Britain's fields had long been dotted with barns but the eighteenth and nineteenth centuries witnessed an explosion in these pragmatic, rural buildings. The country's agriculture was picking up pace – the 'granary of Europe' needed somewhere to thresh and store all its precious wheat, corn and barley. Many of these new barns were built with owl holes, set high in gable ends. These small openings, which let barn owls into the building to roost, marked a change in how the birds were perceived by the men and women who shared their landscape. Far from barn owls being a macabre menace, farmers began to realise that these night-time saviours could protect sacks of grain from four-legged thieves, those mice and rats that gorged themselves when backs were turned. The barn owl became the farmer's ally.

Not everyone learned to love the barn owl, however. Throughout the Victorian era, thousands of barn owls, and other birds of prey, were shot or trapped by keepers who blamed them for attacking game birds. The nineteenth-century obsession with collecting wild birds' eggs and taxidermy also hit the barn owl population hard – few stuffy parlours were complete without a glass-eyed, heart-faced bird trapped under a dome. Only between the First and Second World Wars did anyone think to monitor the nation's barn owl numbers; in 1932, senior civil servant and bird-lover George B. Blaker organised an emergency census and called upon the country to find and record its local owls. It was clear to him that something was amiss: 'The diminishing number of barn (or white) owls in England and Wales in recent years', read the call to arms, 'is giving concern to agriculturists and students of bird life.'[4] Blaker's census estimated a population of 12,000 breeding pairs, which, although unconfirmed, was thought to represent a significant drop in numbers from the early nineteenth century. The barn owl had, at least for a handful of ornithologists and enthusiasts, become a cause for concern.

And yet the general public's relationship with the barn owl is still a peculiar one. While it regularly tops the list of the nation's favourite birds, we seem to admire the barn owl from a cool distance. We like them but we don't *know* them. A brief sighting is a thrill but, as the barn owl is usually a tenant of the night, our paths rarely cross and we leave it at that. And so this book is an attempt to try to tell some of the story of the barn owl's daily – or should that be nightly – life. Few of us know what goes on after dark, underneath the moon, or the journey a barn owl takes from hatchling to full-grown magnificence. Each of the chapters begins with a snapshot of the three months from first pip of the shell to leaving the nest, a fascinating time in the barn owl's early life.

Behind the scenes, there have been some heroic

efforts to protect this glorious creature. As we'll find out later in the book, the twentieth century wasn't kind to barn owls. Changes in farming practices meant that most of the traditional farm buildings that barn owls used disappeared or were converted to housing. The rise of the combine harvester, which leaves much less grain behind in the field than old-fashioned reaping, and the introduction of silos, means that easy gleanings are no longer to be found by some of the barn owl's favourite rodents. Certain pesticides, such as organochlorine, and rodenticides proved lethal for barn owls, causing a dramatic dip in their numbers. Because of the huge increase in the number of motor cars and an ever-expanding road network, traffic accidents have also become a depressingly frequent cause of death for barn owls, killing about a third of all fledglings born every year.

It's difficult to say, with any accuracy, what the numbers are doing. Nocturnal animals are notoriously tricky to study, and count, but most conservation groups agree that while barn owl numbers slumped in the mid-twentieth century, current estimates range between a cautious 4,000 and an optimistic 12,000 breeding pairs in the UK.* America shows a similarly mixed picture – while some states, especially in the south and along the west coast, have good population densities, many places are low on numbers. From New York in the east to North Dakota and Montana, some states have already suffered such losses of barn owl numbers that habitat restoration and nest box programmes may be the only way to bring back any semblance of normality.[5] Knowing more about the barn owl's habitat and habits also gives us ammunition in the conservation battle – we can do things to help, and this book will show you how.

But most of all, this is just the story of a peculiarly beautiful bird. Barn owls are mesmerising. They're also wonderfully unsociable; unlike the nation's garden birds,

---

* In 1987, the Barn Owl Survey of Britain and Ireland recorded 4,450 breeding pairs. Following concerted efforts to restore barn owl numbers, the estimated population today may be as high as 9,000–12,000 pairs.

which can be tempted by a bird table of seeds, the barn owl keeps us at a safe distance. We humans, ever the egocentrics, fancy we see ourselves in the barn owl's big, baby eyes or quizzical tilt of the head. But the barn owl lives on a different plane – a yearly see-saw of feast and famine, companionship and solitude. It seems such a tough life – living in the shadows – but the barn owl has made it this far.

What their future holds, we don't know. Barn owls are known as an 'indicator species' – any increase or decrease in their numbers is an early warning flare that there are bigger issues in the environment. The presence of barn owls in an area is a cause for optimism, a good indicator of biodiversity. Equally, a drop in their numbers can be a danger sign – not only that barn owls are struggling but that other wildlife, which depends on the same habitat, may also be under threat. We know from recent years that the barn owl's success can be undermined by hard winters and very wet springs and summers, all of which affect the amount of prey available to eat. There can be little doubt that extreme weather events, related to climate change, will continue to affect barn owl populations across the world. Their future and ours are inextricably linked.

Or, as Thomas wrote, 'the bird's voice / Speaking for all who lay under the stars'.

Chapter One

FAMILY

It's the beginning of June. The midsummer month.
Named after Juno, the goddess of birth, it's early
summer in all its fresh, ripening glory. In Gaelic,
June is An t'Og mhios – the young month – and high
up in the rafters of an old limestone granary,
a female barn owl stands on a ledge. Next to her,
a clutch of five walnut-sized, china-white eggs
gets a brief airing as she touches each one gently with
her feet and beak. She fusses quietly, nudging
the eggs tight together, before straddling the clutch
and softly settling back down on top of them.
She's been sitting on her eggs for thirty days.
She gets up occasionally to look at the clutch, scratch,
or stretch her wings. But for most of May she's been
in self-imposed isolation, patiently keeping her
eggs warm. The only visitor she gets is another barn
owl, her mate, who dutifully brings regular meals of
a vole or mouse – her prize for maternal diligence.

Under her warm tummy, tiny peeps come from inside one of the eggs. She calls back – a librarian's firm shush – and the egg replies, the baby owl recognising the voice of its parent, even from inside the shell. The pale oval begins to wobble, barely perceptibly, but it's a movement that tells the mother her chick is ready to make an appearance. A tiny chip appears on the surface, then another, and another. With its egg tooth – a small, hard nubbin on the end of its beak – the chick has managed to make a little hole in the shell. All goes quiet for a few hours, until, like a trapped miner regaining his strength, the tap-tapping strikes up again. Slowly, over the night and into the next day, the chick chips away, its writhing, stretching body pushing the crack further apart until finally, like a tea-spooned breakfast egg, the shell hinges open and new life falls, crumpled, into the world.

For a few seconds, the chick – pink and wet with wings unfolding – cries as it clumsily unfurls. The barn owl mother, tidy as always, tosses the unwanted shell to the edge of the ledge and gently hisses her approval. *The effort for the owlet, however, has been nothing short of miraculous and, exhausted, he collapses face down like a spent toddler. Small, helpless and weighing no more than a few sugar lumps, the baby owlet is naked and blind. With the kind of looks that only a mother could love, the newborn chick's long head, fat tummy and big beak look almost comically out of proportion with its tiny wings. For the chick, the hard work is over, but for the mother, the journey has just begun. She knows she, and her mate, have just three months before the owlets will have to leave the safety of the barn and there are so many things to do before their babies – wide-eyed and blinking – must launch, alone, out into the darkness...*

THE BARN OWL FAMILY

The barn owl is a bit of an outsider. Around the world there are over two hundred species of owl and the majority belong to one family, *Strigidae*, or 'typical owls'. The barn owl, however, is different. Thanks to some subtle anatomical differences, taxonomists put barn owls in their own special category – the *Tytonidae* family – a group thought to have diverged from typical owls around 45 million years ago.[6]

For the casual observer, only one of these differences is easy to spot – barn owls have heart-shaped faces rather than round ones, like typical owls. There are other distinctions too, which are trickier to see. The eyes of barn owls are proportionally smaller than other species, and their feet are slightly different too. Get a little more intimate with the barn owl's anatomy and you'd also find they have a longer beak than other owls, compared to their body size, and, unlike other owls, its wishbone is joined to its breastbone.

Owl taxonomy is a moving target and the barn owl used to be classed as one species, with thirty-six different sub-species distributed all around the world. Recent DNA sequencing has changed all that and some subspecies have been reclassified as new species in their own right. The American subspecies of barn owl *alba pratincole*, for example, is now the separate species American barn owl (*Tyto furcata*).

With the *Tytonidae* family, some are native to vast land masses, such as the American barn owl (*Tyto furcata*) or the dark-breasted barn owl (*Tyto alba guttata*), which dominates central and eastern Europe. Others have colonised only a small, ecological niche – such as Curaçao's short-winged Caribbean (*Tyto alba bargei*) or the petite barn owl of the Galapagos Islands (*Tyto alba punctatissima*). The *Tytonidae* family has also lost many of its subspecies over time. Around five million years ago, for example, the Mediterranean had at least two now extinct barn owl subspecies – *Tyto robusta* and *Tyto gigantea*. The names are a giveaway – they were, apparently, absolute whoppers. While *robusta* was about 65cm (26in) high – about twice the size of a modern barn owl – *gigantea* was even bigger at just shy of a metre (39in).

No one really knows why the barn owl has been, evolutionarily speaking, such a triumph. There are a number of traits, however, that would have certainly helped the bird spread its wings across the world. The first is that barn owls don't specialise in one type of prey, giving them a flexibility and opportunism that many other bird species lack. From region to region, they've adapted to local menus – whether it's mice or marsupials, rats or large insects. Another reason might be that, for a large bird, barn owls have a lot of babies. The barn owl will begin breeding in its first year and, in the right circumstances, can produce two or, very occasionally, three broods a year. And while the average brood is around four or five chicks, it's not unknown for barn owls to raise eight, nine or even ten owlets in one nest. Compared to a peregrine falcon, which lays three or four eggs a year in total, the barn owl can be a startlingly prolific bird.

One of the more complex reasons for the barn owl's success, however, is its relationship with people. Barn owls are one of the few birds to have benefited, at least initially, from human activities. When agriculture first appeared, around 10,000–12,000 years ago, the barn owl managed to exploit the new ecological niche that was created when forests were cleared to grow food. Not only did the absence of trees make it easier for barn owls to access open ground but the presence of cereal crops actually boosted the number of rodents scuttling around on the ground. And although barn owls originally evolved to nest in cliff cavities and tree hollows, human settlements, with their churches, farms and other buildings, offered an enticing array of places to roost and raise a family. The fact that barn owls come out when humans are in bed may have also helped with their survival – shooting a bird in the daylight is far easier than taking potshots in the fading light.

THE WESTERN BARN OWL

Most of this book will focus on the Western barn owl (*Tyto alba alba*), a gloriously snow-breasted bird found across much of western and southern Europe. Stretching from Britain in the north to Morocco in the south, Portugal in the west and Greece in the east, the Western barn owl has put down its roots anywhere there is open countryside. It also tends to prefer lowlands, places with mild climates that don't get prolonged periods of snow. As we'll see later, snow cover makes hunting for small mammals incredibly time-consuming and barn owl numbers often take a steep downturn during bad winters. Barn owls are also badly insulated and lose lots of body heat during cold weather. One of the most surprising things about the barn owl, an icon of the chilly British countryside, is that the bird most probably evolved in Australasia – a climate both much warmer and drier than our own. Barn owls, therefore, have to run the gauntlet every winter – between December and early spring – and often struggle to find enough food to see them through the most energy-sapping period of the year.

In the UK, if you're lucky, you might also get a glimpse of the continental dark-breasted barn owl (*Tyto alba guttata*); although barn owls are not migratory birds, they have been known to occasionally make it across the sea between eastern England and north-east Europe. Dark-breasted barn owls have been recorded in

East Anglia and East Yorkshire, for example, where they freely mate with our own Western barn owls; and like any good foreign exchange programme, Britain's barn owls have also been known to make the return journey.[7]

Unlike many other owls, who prefer secretive woodland, the barn owl is traditionally a bird of open grassland, savannah and wetlands, places where it can use its hearing, eyesight and spellbinding aerial skills to full effect. In the UK, where little lowland wilderness remains, the barn owl has managed to carve out a place for itself that makes use of the landscape created by traditional mixed farming; in the absence of large areas of wild grassland, the barn owl survives by hunting along the rough margins at the edges of farmers' fields, woodland rides, road verges, open ditches and hedgerows. Slightly scruffy, sparsely populated rural sites are also popular – unprepossessing places such as military ranges, derelict airfields, ruins and unkempt parkland can often provide ample hunting and undisturbed nesting opportunities.

Did you know?

Ever wondered which owl you were hearing in the darkness? The tawny owl (Strix aluco) makes the cartoon-like 'twit-twoo' most of us are familiar with. The female tawny owl calls 'Toowit Toowit', and the male replies 'Hoo, HooHooHooHoooooo'. If you hear a short, repetitive 'wuuh', it's probably a little owl (Athene noctua). The barn owl, on the other hand, makes a range of calls from an eerie 'Screeeeech' to food-begging shushes 'Pushhhh Pushhhh', but definitely no hooting. Spring is the best time to hear barn owls; listen out for prolonged, one-note, piercing screams in the darkness – it's probably a male barn owl trying to woo a female.

VITAL STATISTICS

From a distance, the Western barn owl looks an imposing bird. Appearances can be deceptive, however. Although its average height is around 35cm (14in), with a wingspan at around 90cm (35in), the barn owl is an incredibly slight creature underneath all that plumage.

Most adults only weigh about 300–360g (11–12oz), the same as a three-week-old kitten.

As a general rule, female barn owls are slightly heavier than males, but this varies throughout the year. For most of the time, females weigh about 30–60g (1–2oz) more than their mates. At the beginning of the year, however, the female barn owl starts to eat increasing amounts in preparation for breeding, putting on an extra third in body weight to see her through spring and early summer. Males, on the other hand, maintain a fairly consistent weight through the year, apart from a brief drop in midsummer when they're working extra hard to feed their adolescent offspring.

The most striking feature of the barn owl, however, is its pale colouring. 'Tyto alba' means 'white owl' and, over the years, the bird has attracted many a folk name – White Hoolet, Ghost Owl, Gilly White, Silver Owl – inspired by its waxen looks. In reality, the bird is more subtly shaded than that. Flying overhead, we're dazzled by the snowy chest and underwings, but perched and still, the Western barn owl is also washed head to tail with golds and buff greys. Barn owls across the globe also come in a subtle range of hues – from ghostly greys to rich, reddish browns. Researchers are still trying to understand why such variation exists, and it was long thought that different coloured plumage may relate to local differences in diet, foraging behaviour and other environmental constraints.[8]

A new study, however, recently may have found the answer to why barn owls in the UK are white-breasted and those in central and eastern Europe are brown breasted. During the last Ice Age, different species of barn owl took refuge in the warmer parts of southern Europe. As this glacial period came to an end, and temperatures gradually increased, the barn owl began to venture north again. It used to be thought that barn owl (*Tyto alba*) only gained its white coloration after it had reached Great Britain but genetics now show us that the bird came directly from a white-coloured population in the Iberian Peninsula.[9]

Did you know?
A rare gene mutation can occasionally lead to a barn owl being born covered with black feathers. These beautiful, one-in-a-hundred-thousand birds are called 'melanistic barn owls' and usually don't survive in the wild as they are starved or killed by parents who are confused by the colouration. There are, however, a handful who have survived in captivity.

Male and female barn owls also look slightly different, although sexing owls by their feather colours isn't an exact science. Broadly speaking, females are often a darker buff colour, with stripier feathers, and tiny spots flecked over their chest and under the wings. Males are generally lighter and don't tend to have any spots on their pure-white chests and underwings. Confusingly, with the interbreeding that's going on between the *Tyto alba alba* and the dark-breasted *guttata*, it's becoming increasingly more common to find male barn owls with flecks and darker chests. Interestingly, there has been some research into why female barn owls have spots and, more importantly, why males seem to prefer the most spotted females. One study found a connection between a female's 'spottiness' and her resistance to parasites – the greater the proportion of plumage covered by dots, the greater the female's natural resistance to certain disease-causing pests. No correlation was found, however, between male spottiness and parasitic resistance.[10]

Life in the wild is tough and barn owls rarely live to enjoy their old age. In captivity, barn owls can reach twenty years and upwards but, battling against the elements out in nature, few see more than four winters. Infant mortality is also high – of those that fledge, nearly three-quarters die in their first year.

Did you know?

Barn owls don't live that long out in nature but there have been some notable old-timers: Bernice, the oldest recorded British barn owl living in the wild, reached a remarkable fifteen years, while Barny, the most senior resident in UK captivity, managed a full three decades.***

HOME RANGES

Every barn owl has its home range. This is a defined area where it hunts for food, roosts and, during the breeding season, nests. The size of the home range varies, depending whether the barn owl is alone or feeding its family. When a barn owl is nesting, 90 per cent of its

* *'Bernice', recorded by Bisham Barn Owl Group, Buckinghamshire. Hatch date 2001.*

** *'Barny', recorded by The Barn Owl Centre in Gloucestershire. Hatch date 1986.*

foraging seems to occur within a 1km radius (3.14 km²) but for the rest of the year it can extend up to 50 km².

Outside of the breeding season, which in the UK can run from as early as February and finish as late as October (if there is a second brood), the barn owl isn't tied to the nest. This means he or she can fly further to find food, especially in the winter months when they need to exploit a declining food supply. In Britain, barn owls also seem to stick to their home ranges year after year, only occasionally moving on if a partner dies, the site is disturbed, or food becomes scarce. Even then, barn owls are creatures of habit and are far more likely to die than move. Across the rest of the world, the picture is less clear – some barn owls are very site loyal while others change their home ranges year after year. Quite why this is, we don't really know.

Within the home range are places that are special to the barn owl. The bird will have a number of hunting areas it prefers, a nest site and a handful of regular roosting places:

Nests

Barn owls don't actually build nests. Instead, they prefer to find a cavity or dry ledge, hidden and high off the ground. Before buildings were an option, barn owls would nest in a range of places – crevices in cliff faces, tree hollows or caves. Man-made structures, however, have proved popular and barn owls set up home in a wide range of constructions, from barns to church towers, haystacks to roof voids. In more recent years, nest boxes have replaced many of the old trees and buildings that no longer exist. Estimates suggest that as many as three-quarters of all Britain's barn owls now nest in purpose-built boxes.[11] As a species, however, barn owls aren't hugely territorial. And while a male barn owl will valiantly guard his mate near the nest, out and about barn owls seem to leave each other in peace. Home ranges are also not mutually exclusive – one barn owl's range can overlap with another's. Conflicts are few and far between.

Roosts

Barn owls do a lot of resting. In the middle of the day, when they're off duty, barn owls will fly to one of a few favourite roosting sites and doze. Between late afternoon and early morning, when the owl is in hunting mode, the barn owl will return to a roosting site for a brief respite or to shelter from the weather. Roosting sites don't have to be as big as nesting sites – just a hole in a tree, a gap in a hay stack or a covered ledge will do. Barn owls also occasionally share roosts – a barn owl 'husband and wife' may occupy the same roosting site even out of breeding season and it's not unknown for barn owls to roost communally, albeit in small numbers. Why they do this isn't clear but there might be benefits from sharing a snoozing space, such as keeping watch for other birds or predators, staying warm in poor weather, or help finding a mate.[12] When barn owls have been tracked with GPS systems, it seems to show that they use different roosts depending on the time of day. One study showed that, in the breeding season, the male barn owl roosted close to the nest during the day and further afield at night. The owls also seemed to have a number of 'commutes' – a handful of favourite direct routes between hunting grounds and the nest.

Did you know?

You won't see a barn owl carrying a twig in its beak or plumping a comfy woven nest with soft material. Often just a dry ledge in a barn will do, or a flat-bottomed hollow in a tree, and barn owls will often revisit a nesting site year after year. The barn owl may make use of the previous year's nest debris – the layers of old pellets and other detritus – and scratch a shallow depression where the eggs will sit. That's why barn owl nests are sometimes referred to as 'scrapes'.

Chapter Two

BODY

Three weeks have passed since the first owlet
emerged from his shell. Today is summer solstice,
the longest day of the year, and the sun has reached her
highest point in the sky. It's been a glorious cloudless
day but, as dusk falls, the stone ledge in the barn
comes alive with the sound of squabbling.

Since the first chick arrived, four more have followed.
Each owlet broke out of its shell two days apart
from the next; unlike other birds, barn owls lay their
eggs in staggered intervals, forty-eight hours apart.
There's ten days' difference between the youngest
and the eldest chick – both in age and size.
By the time the fifth baby owl hatched, the first
had already ballooned in size. The disparity in body
size can look alarming – like Russian dolls,
the five chicks could practically stack inside each
other – and in times of extreme hardship it's not
uncommon for the bigger siblings to prey on their
smaller, weaker brothers and sisters.

*Thankfully, the weather has been kind – not too
much rain and plenty of warm, mild evenings –
and there's talonfuls of food being ferried from
the fields to the nest by both parents. The mother
has started to leave her brood in short bursts, joining
her mate in their endless trolley-dash for small
mammals to bring back for their voracious offspring.
The chicks have a thicker coat of downy feathers
now, which will keep them warm even when they're
unattended. Each of the owlets needs four feeds a day –
about 60g (2oz) of food in all – the equivalent of three
plump voles or six shrews. Tracking down dozens
of tiny rodents, plus enough to fill your own stomach,
is a time-consuming business; the parents have
to be smart – they'll catch and keep the smallest,
least nutritious prey for themselves out in the field and
bring the fattest, juiciest finds back to the nest. This
way, they can save precious time and energy, keeping
the number of home visits to a minimum.*

The mother returns to the ledge with a vole.
At her arrival, the chicks frantically try to attract
her attention, rasping and wheezing for food.
By now, the oldest of the chicks can swallow
a whole shrew or small mouse but the younger
ones still need their meals tearing into tiny pieces.
For the first twenty or so days of all the owlets' lives,
the mother will feed her babies by leaning over
their heads with a tempting morsel and gently
touching the base of their beaks to encourage
the chicks to open their mouths.

At three weeks old, our first chick is also starting
to take in much more of his surroundings. He's grown
spectacularly quickly – in just over twenty days
he's reached nearly 10cm (4in) in height and put on
the kind of weight gain most body builders would envy.
From a one-day-old 20g (¾oz) scrap, the barn owl
chick is now twelve times heavier at nearly

a quarter of a kilogram, growing into a fat, white-
feathered Bramley apple in just a few short weeks.
Everything is still out of proportion though –
it's hard to imagine that this cumbersome chick,
with his tiny head and floppy, drunkard's wings is only
weeks away from physical perfection...

❦

THE BARN OWL'S EARS

Barn owls are both nocturnal and crepuscular, meaning they hunt not only at night but also at dusk and dawn. And while a hungry barn owl will even venture out in broad daylight, the bird is primarily a creature most comfortable with low light, where it can hunt alone, unbothered by other birds and predators. When you stalk in the darkness, like the barn owl, the primary sense you rely on is hearing. The barn owl's ears and auditory system are spectacularly good – an evolutionary adaptation that has enabled them to dominate the night.

To understand how the barn owl's ears work, it's important to know why they need them. Barn owls use their hearing to detect prey on the ground and, in many cases, pinpoint small mammals that are hidden, even in the moonlight, in the undergrowth or snow. Without anything to visually lock on to, the barn owl relies on picking up the most minute of noises – the almost imperceptible rustles and squeaks made by their prey.

Working in poor light or total blackness, the barn owl's head needs to do two things: the first is to pick up, like a radar, as much sound as possible; and the second is to work out which direction the sound is coming from. The barn owl's whole head is designed for listening. Its face is large and covered with layers of stiff feathers arranged in tightly packed rows. This is called the 'facial ruff' and, like a satellite dish, is brilliant at picking up high-frequency sounds. Like a cupped hand, the ruff channels and amplifies the sound towards the barn owl's ears, which are hidden under the feathers at the side of the head. Their Roman-nose-like beak also pushes the sound towards each ear.

When the owl hears a noise, it's able to detect which direction the sound is coming from. The sound hitting either the left ear first or the right will tell the bird where the prey is located horizontally – the owl's ears are so sensitive that it can pick up a left/right time difference of as little as 30 millionths of a second. What's even more astonishing is that the barn owl's ears are slightly asymmetrical – one is slightly higher than the other. This remarkable adaptation allows the barn owl to work out where sound is coming from in the vertical plane. If the barn owl hears a mouse rustling in the grass below, for instance, that sound will hit the ear closest to the ground first. The barn owl then moves its head until the sound arrives at both ears at the same time. Using this left-right, up-down location system like a gun's crosshair sight, the barn owl's brain can create a mental image of where the prey is and lock on to its target with lethal efficiency.

The barn owl's supreme hearing is used right up until the moment of capture. In fact, scientists have shown that when the barn owl swoops in for its kill, the bird actually reorientates its talons to align with the body of the mouse. It isn't doing this by sight but as a result of the owl detecting miniscule changes in the sounds created by the prey that tell the bird which direction the prey is travelling.[13] Studies of the brain have also shown that the owl's *medulla* – the part of the brain linked to hearing – is more complex than those in other birds. The barn owl's *medulla* compared to the crow's, for example, has three times as many neurons.[14]

In fact, the barn owl's hearing is so good it can hunt in total darkness. In a now-famous experiment, American scientist Roger Payne wanted to discover more about how barn owls located their prey. People had wondered whether the barn owl was using extra senses – such as smell or infrared detection – to find its prey in the dark, but Payne wasn't convinced. In the experiment, the barn owl was first allowed to catch a live mouse in a completely dark room – the floor of the chamber was covered in leaves, which rustled with every movement the mouse made, and the barn owl caught it with ease. When a mouse-sized piece of paper was then dragged across the floor, instead of a live mouse, the barn owl still attempted to catch it – suggesting to Payne that it could only hear, but not see or smell, what it was hunting. This theory was confirmed when other tests showed that if a mouse was walking along in complete darkness, towing a piece of rustling paper behind it, the barn owl would attempt to catch the noisier of the two objects: i.e. the paper, not the mouse.[15] Sound, it was proved, was the barn owl's primary cue.

The only downside of this hearing superpower may be that, in noisy environments, detecting prey might be difficult. Windy and stormy days are challenging enough but human-generated sounds, such as busy roads, industry or loud music, may seriously interfere with the barn owl's ability to use its exceptional hearing. One study, which looked at the effect of an industrial gas plant's noise on the hunting success of owls, found that for each decibel increase in noise, the bird's ability to locate and strike prey decreased by 8 per cent.[16] That's nearly a one in ten drop in hunting success. If a barn owl, attempting to feed a family of five chicks, experienced this kind of dip in its food catches, it would result in one of their owlets only receiving half the nutrition it needed and failing to thrive.

Did you know?

Barn owls retain excellent hearing throughout their lives. Human hearing deteriorates as we age, especially when it comes to sounds at high frequency. Barn owls have 'ageless' ears – their bodies repair any damage to their auditory cells regardless of the age of the bird. The theory is that humans, and all other mammals, lost this regenerative ability somewhere along the line, while barn owls – who rely almost solely on their hearing – kept this evolutionary quirk.[17]

SILENT FLIGHT

One of the barn owl's neatest tricks is its almost entirely soundless flight. For the bird, being silent on the wing offers an incredible advantage when it comes to its evening patrol – not only does it allow the barn owl to sneak up on unsuspecting prey, it also means the animal's acute hearing is not distracted by the sound of its own beating wings.

To achieve aeronautical silence, the barn owl uses

two cunning adaptations. The first is to have wings that are relatively big compared to its lightweight, slender body. A barn owl's wings are about two and a half times larger than those of other birds of the same size[18] and generate plenty of lift without it having to furiously flap its wings. Indeed, the barn owl's flying movements are so economical that just one single wing beat will allow it to glide effortlessly through the air. Its large wings also allow the barn owl to fly slowly – at times it can look like the bird almost stalls mid-flight. Slow and steady wins the day, with the barn owl able to drop out of the sky on to its prey at a moment's notice.

The barn owl's feathers are also different from other birds. When air rushes over most birds' beating wings, it makes a characteristic 'flapping' noise created by air turbulence – think of the frantic fluttering of a pigeon's wings as it bursts into flight. Barn owls have evolved flight feathers with tiny comb-like fringes along the edges, which seem to dampen down any noise generated by turbulence. The barn owl's wings also have a super-soft velvet-like surface, which helps reduce the noise and absorb any sounds made by the feathers when they move against each other.[19]

To enjoy all the privileges of silent flight, however, the barn owl made a devil's bargain. In return for its soft, noise-absorbing feathers, the barn owl traded its ability to fly effectively in the rain. Their fluffy plumage isn't very waterproof and gets easily waterlogged in a downpour. Only a desperate barn owl will attempt a flight in poor weather and a prolonged wet summer can be as disastrous for the population as a cold, harsh winter. The endless sorties also take a toll on the barn owl's plumage and so, from time to time, its feathers will be replaced. The ones that really matter are the flight feathers – known as the 'primaries' – the longest feathers on the bird's wing and the furthest away from its body when its wings are outstretched. The barn owl has ten of these primaries, plus a hidden eleventh one, numbered from primary one (which is nearest the body) to primary ten (nearest the wing tip).

To keep the bird flightworthy throughout the year, there has to be a reliable timetable for primary feathers to drop. And so barn owls have developed a particular sequence or 'moult strategy', which allows certain primaries to be replaced at certain times. From the moment of hatching to the following year's breeding season, the young barn owl will keep all its new flight feathers. The following year, it will only replace one particular flight feather – primary six (although sometimes primary seven too). In the next year, it will replace primaries five and seven (the feathers either side of primary six), and the following year primaries eight, four and three.[20] The cycle finishes in the final year with primary feathers nine, ten and one.*

This sequential moulting allows barn owl experts to estimate the age of a bird. To do this, a handler needs to gently extend the barn owl's wing and check for the position of new feathers, which are whiter and shinier than the dulled, older primaries. Interestingly, male and female barn owls typically moult at different times

* The barn owl's soft, small body feathers and its tail feathers are also annually moulted but not in any predictably sequential way.

– growing new feathers takes up valuable energy so the female will begin moulting when she's nesting. Males, on the other hand, wait until the exhausting business of baby-rearing is over and will start to moult when the owlets begin to fend for themselves in late summer. Single male owls, footloose and fancy free, without any family to look after, will start to lose their feathers earlier in the year.

One of the perennial questions about barn owls surrounds its feather colours. Why does a bird that hunts in low light have such a pale body and wings? Surely a camouflaged, dark plumage would have conferred the barn owl an advantage if it was prowling the skies in the darkness? The other famously white owl, the snowy owl, has colourless feathers to help it blend into the frozen landscape. Barn owls don't occupy that environmental niche and never have done – in temperate countries, their white plumage sticks out like a sore thumb, even in the dead of night. Furthermore, the whitest part of the barn owl is its underside – its belly and underwings – the area most likely to be seen by prey looking up from ground level. To add to the mystery, barn owls seem to hunt even better under the reflective, bright light of a full moon – the very conditions that will stop the bird blending into the gloom.

The answer to this riddle was recently solved. Researchers discovered that the glaring whiteness of the barn owl's plumage actually helps the owl stun its prey. As moonlight bounces off the barn owl's pale feathers, the effect on rodents is similar to that of a rabbit caught in headlights – it triggers a freezing response. The experiment also showed that the brighter the light, and therefore the more dazzling the feathers, the longer the prey was glued to the spot, making it easier to catch. Other studies have shown that barn owls' success rates are much higher if their prey is standing still; stationary rodents will be caught nine times out of ten but a mouse on the move will only be captured one in every five attempts.[21] And while full moon conditions were optimal for barn owl hunting success, even on a partially moonlit night the barn owl's plumage could still help paralyse its prey. Rodents have a well-known aversion to bright light – the barn owl is simply exploiting this natural trait.[22]

Did you know?
Barn owls have a canny trick to help keep their feathers looking shipshape. By the age of about two, adult barn owls have developed a special middle 'toe' on their feet – called a pectinate claw – which has serrated edges like a comb. The barn owl uses this special talon to groom the feathers on its head – the only place it can't preen with its beak – and scratch off any bothersome lice. Most birds don't have this adaptation, but barn owls need it because they often pick up parasites from their rodent prey.

NIGHT SIGHT

Unlike other owls, who have very large yellowy-orange eyes, barn owl eyes are relatively small and dark, like chocolate buttons. Barn owls, like all birds of prey, have front-facing eyes – this allows them to use their binocular vision (the ability to see an object with both eyes at the same time) to help them judge distance when locating prey. Front-facing, binocular eyes, however, only give barn owls a visual field of about 110 degrees – this is the range of what they can see at any one time. Birds who have eyes on the sides of their head have a much bigger visual field of about 300 degrees – a difference explained by their feeding strategies. Prey animals such as sparrows often have wide visual fields to help them detect danger approaching from all angles. Predators like the barn owl don't need a particularly wide field of vision, as they are the hunter not the hunted, and instead rely on their sharp-eyed ability to spot a meal even at long distance.

The barn owl doesn't have eyeballs as such; instead, their eyes are tube-like and fixed in their sockets. Humans can roll and move their eyes, but barn owls compensate for this lack of mobility by moving their entire heads through an impressive 270 degrees. If a human attempted that, we would cut off the blood supply to our brains and faint. Barn owls have a special adaptation in their neck vertebrae, however, that makes sure the blood vessels don't get crushed when they twist their heads.

Barn owls also bob their heads up and down and side to side – a trick that can look comical to the casual observer. This swaying head movement helps the barn owl quickly work out the distance and depth of an object thanks to a phenomenon called 'motion parallax'. If you gazed out of a window at a point far in the distance and moved your head from side to side, you'd notice something peculiar; anything in your field of vision closer than the distant focus point appears to move more dramatically than the focus point. The closer the object to your eyes, the more it moves when you move your head from side to side. This difference in movement cleverly allows the barn owl to estimate how far away an object is.

To allow the barn owl to see in dim light, its eyes have enlarged corneas and lenses to let in as much light as possible. The barn owl also has a reflective layer of tissue behind the retina that bounces light around the eye. Acting like a mirror, the *tapetum lucidum* dramatically increases the amount of light that reaches the barn owl's retina. This 'eyeshine' feature is also present in other animals who come out in the dark; from cats to deer, dogs to racoons, the *tapetum lucidum* is what makes their eyes appear to glow in the glare of a headlight and inspired eccentric Yorkshire inventor Percy Shaw to create reflective road studs or 'cat's eyes' in the 1930s.

At the back of the eye, the barn owl also has more light-sensitive cells than colour-sensitive ones – the retina has a very high density of rods that are extremely receptive to even the lowest levels of light, helping objects in the dark to appear brighter than they would to the human eye. There's only so much space on the retina, however, and the barn owl doesn't have many cells that can detect colour differences. This has prompted scientists to conclude that barn owls see in limited colour or monochrome and are probably long-sighted, excelling at detecting prey at a distance rather than relying on close-up detail. Tests have shown that the barn owl can outcompete both cats and humans in its ability to see in the dark but, come the bright daylight, the human, falcon, eagle and even pigeon outperform the barn owl. What's worth remembering, however, is that eyesight isn't particularly critical to the barn owl's hunting success. A barn owl's eyesight is good, especially in low light, but its hearing is even better. Research has shown that barn owls can capture prey even when blindfolded – if they can't hear or they lose their facial disc feathers, however, they're in real trouble.

Did you know?

It used to be thought that barn owls visually track their prey, constantly keeping their focus on the unsuspecting creature as it scuttles along. New research suggests that the barn owls use a more complex technique, where they calculate an interception point based on the direction and speed of the prey. Barn owls seem to work out where they think the prospective 'clash point' will be and then return their attention to the target – predicting where the mammal will be when the owl plans to strike. In response, some small mammals, such as voles, try to confuse the barn owl by stopping and starting, or 'freezing and fleeing', so that the bird has to constantly re-estimate the final target point.[23]

THE BARN OWL BRAIN

The barn owl brain is, like that of many other species, poorly understood. Popular culture hasn't helped – we seem to lump them into either the 'wise old owl' category, based on their ever watchful, human-like faces, or dismiss the barn owl as 'bird-brained', with all its other avian cousins. When we use the insult 'bird brain', we're describing someone who's stupid, flighty and inattentive. On this point we could not be more wrong. Studies have repeatedly shown that barn owls have a superior ability to concentrate. Like many other highly focused predatory birds, barn owls can quickly judge from a busy scene the most important piece of information on which to hone in. This kind of single-mindedness requires the barn owl's brain to be able to pay close attention to the thing it needs to look at but also actively suppress all the other, superfluous content – an ability called 'distractor suppression'.

Other studies have also shown that the barn owl shares an important mental ability with humans and primates. A fundamental part of perception is being able to tell one object from another or distinguish an object from its background. One of the ways that people do this is to group elements together within a scene to try to make sense of the whole – such as a cluster of sheep against a hillside or a flock of birds in the sky. Sometimes that object is by itself – a bird in a tree, for example, or a mouse scuttling across a carpet. Scientists have long believed this type of visual processing requires a complex brain, the kind found in humans and primates. But a recent scientific study of barn owls tested their ability to locate a moving target among varied and changing backgrounds and discovered that barn owls also have this type of visual processing.

Did you know?
In Hindi, the word ulloo *means owl but is also used as a slang word to mean a 'fool' because the bird sleeps through the day and only comes out when the rest of the world has gone to sleep.*

Chapter Three

FOOD

It's mid-July. It's been an uncharacteristically hot,
sultry few weeks and nature is losing her patience.
These are the 'dog days' – named after Sirius,
the dog star, and its position in the heavens.
For the ancient Greeks, Sirius was thought to behave
like an extra sun, doubling the heat from the sky
and upending the weather with its drought,
thunderstorms and feverish temperatures.

In the shade of the limestone barn, however,
the outside world – with its charms and curses
– is a place yet to be discovered by the owlets.
Their days and nights are busy enough – life seems
to be a never-ending nursery cycle of eating, napping
and playing. The eldest chick is now six weeks
old and gloriously fat. At nearly 400g (14oz)
but only 20cm (8in) tall, he's a giant, overindulged
toddler, heavier than either of his parents and
wonderfully rotund, like an Easter egg on legs.
His weight has now peaked and will drop slightly

before he leaves home, but overfeeding is all part
of the strategy – the owlet is going to need plenty of
puppy fat reserves to power his final growth spurt
and produce a fine complement of flight feathers.

All the nestlings are a handful. Most of their eating
is done during the cover of darkness, with both mother
and father spending the night searching for food.
The chicks have perfected a food-begging hiss – pushhh,
pushhh, pushhh – a sound that never fails to grab
the attention of a parent returning with a mouse in
its beak. And while meals are largely an evening affair,
during the daylight hours the chicks are also awake
between naps. Unlike humans, who enjoy one
long rest between sunset and sunrise, owlets sleep
in short bursts – throughout the day and night,
the chicks may be awake for just a minute or so
and then catch a twenty-second snooze; and while
this might seem like a recipe for unrefreshing sleep,
this rapid awake/snooze cycle helps the chicks
constantly keep an eye out for danger.

At this age, the owlets are starting to discover their voices and bodies – like eager puppies, they play-act, pouncing, wobbling and jumping around the nest. They've also become potty-trained, leaving their droppings on the edge of their nest area. The chicks are starting to preen their own feathers, flap and even annoy each other with the occasional wilful peck. One of their greatest discoveries, however, is their head mobility. As well as constantly bobbing and swaying their heads, the owlets can now dial their faces upside down through 180 degrees, a party trick they practise with great aplomb. In just the last few days, the babies have started to look just that little bit more grown up. Their faces are beginning to morph into that unmistakable, angelic heart shape and a few promising buff flight feathers are starting to peek through their baby white down...

🌹

DIET

Across the world, small mammals make up the majority of the barn owl's diet. There's significant regional variation, however, and barn owls make the most of local conditions, catching and killing a number of different creatures from voles to mice, marsupials to crickets. Bird-rich environments, such as islands, can provide an abundant alternative to rodents for the barn owl, while in places short on squeaks, the barn owl is known to adapt to eating large insects, amphibians and reptiles.

In the UK, the barn owl's favourite prey is the field vole (*Microtus agrestis*), which constitutes nearly half of its diet. Common shrews make up a fifth of the barn owl's meals, as do wood mice, with the rest of their nutrition coming from a diverse range of small mammals including pygmy shrews, bank voles, house mice and brown rats. Small birds are caught over the cooler months, when small mammals are more difficult to find, while frogs occasionally make it on to the menu in springtime, when they're moving to new spawning grounds. In fact, the British barn owl's diet changes throughout the year, depending on what's most abundant. Like an eco-conscious shopper, the barn owl eats seasonally and sustainably, taking advantage of prey abundance and what's locally available.

In many cases, the barn owl is forced to shift from one major food source to another, with seasonal fluctuations. Different small mammals breed, flourish and make themselves vulnerable to barn owls at different times of the year. In Britain, small mammal reproduction picks up pace in April but the real period of abundance is between June and October, when the countryside is particularly rich with voles, mice and shrews. This allows the barn owl to feed its growing

young on as wide and varied a diet as possible, just when they need it the most. Later in the year, when small mammal numbers decline or they become less active, barn owls occasionally raid autumn roosts for birds and, over the winter months, historically made the most of grain barns infested with rodents. In springtime, male voles are an easy catch – during their breeding season they come out to defend their territories, squeaking loudly and having brawls with other voles.[24] Wood mice don't hibernate and, if there's a good supply of food, will continue to have multiple litters of between four and eight baby mice right through the year, providing the barn owl with a potential source of meals over the winter months. Similarly, small birds are known to be taken when little else is available – bird remains found in the pellets of a number of British barn owls read like a Who's Who of garden favourites including house sparrows, starlings, finches, chaffinches, thrushes, blackbirds, robins, skylarks and warblers.[25]

Did you know?

Barn owls are well known for swooping on to prey on the ground, but they have very occasionally been known to catch a meal mid-air. In the UK, bats represent only 0.03 per cent of the barn owl's diet but researchers in northern Germany found an unusually high percentage of bat bones in local barn owl pellets. The birds were hunting the Natterer's bat (Myotis nattereri) in extraordinarily high numbers, making up about a third of their diet. The bats must have been caught during flight, the study concluded, because the barn owls couldn't get access to the narrow spaces where the bats were sleeping.[26]

Barn owls like to swallow their prey whole. They can't process bone and so the barn owl has to regurgitate any it ingests. Smaller, therefore, is definitely better, so the barn owl focuses its energies on tiny mammals. Even when it pursues bulkier rodents – such as brown rats – the barn owl will tend to pick off the smaller, immature ones rather than the full-grown adults. The barn owl eats on average just over 75–100g (2½–3½oz) of food a day but females can scoff substantially more, especially when breeding or preparing to breed. Larger subspecies of barn owl also consume more than this – the North American barn owl, for example, eats nearer 150g (5oz) per day on average.[27]

There are other benefits to hunting large numbers of tiny creatures rather than relying on one big meal a day. Larger prey is often stronger and would cost the barn owl more in energy to subdue; if a barn owl tackled a heftier animal – such as a cat or a hare – it would risk being hurt itself in the attack or discover that the creature had a feistier self-defence strategy than the bird anticipated. The barn owl needs to have as short a handling time as possible between catching its prey, carrying it and digesting it. And while small rodents can be popped down the gullet like pills, it takes significant time and energy to dispatch and dissect larger prey using only a beak and talons.

One experiment, for example, which offered barn owls a range of prey of various sizes, showed that most of the time the birds would only tackle rats up to 80g (3oz) in weight – bigger rats proved formidable opponents in battle and defended themselves fiercely.[28] Larger prey also takes more energy to carry home and makes the barn owl a more attractive target for prey robbery – when other birds mob the barn owl and attempt to steal its meal. The study concluded that the ideal weight for a catch was between 10g and 40g (⅓–1½oz) – smaller than that and the barn owl wasted its energy hunting what is effectively only a snack; bigger than that and the risks of a failed attack were too high. Interestingly, the experiment also found that barn owls will take a chance on larger prey if they're really struggling for food or their intended victim is compromised in some way, i.e. injured, young or elderly.

PELLETS

Barn owls have proved so efficient at eating large volumes of small vermin that they are increasingly being deployed as agents of natural pest control. From vineyards on the west coast of America to fields and orchards in Israel, farmers and growers are being encouraged to erect barn owl nest boxes instead of using costly and environmentally harmful chemicals to tackle the local rodent population. It's a symbiotic solution and an effective one, especially if you do the maths. If an adult barn owl eats four small mammals in a day, that's nearly 1,500 a year. If that barn owl is also part of a family, and not only feeding itself but another parent and five owlets, that's anywhere between 4,000 and 9,000 potential prey items a year, making a significant difference to a farm's pest problem. The barn owl, it seems, is finding its agricultural niche once more.

In one case study, researchers counted and extrapolated the number of rodents being caught by barn owls nesting in California's Napa Valley wine region. Results indicated that each barn owl family, in each nest box, was eating between around 2,000 and 8,000 rodents a year. Testing to see whether the rodents were being taken from the surrounding countryside, rather than the grounds of the vineyards, the study also tracked where the prey was being caught and killed. The nest boxes were surrounded not just by vineyards but also grassland, forest and other wild habitat. The 40 per cent of land that was vineyards gave the barn owls about 40 per cent of their prey – a result that showed barn owls were as happy to hunt among the grapevines as any other nearby landscape.[29]

Did you know?

A British study that looked at barn owl eating habits found that 90 per cent of the bird's diet was made up of rodents and shrews; there were, however, some occasional surprises including young moles, baby rabbits, weasels, toads, bats, beetles, earwigs and even the odd earthworm (a food eaten with relish by both little owls and tawny owls but only very rarely by the barn owl). The study also collected anecdotal evidence of an ill-fated encounter when a barn owl attempted to catch a stoat, a foolhardy mission that sadly ended in the deaths of both predators.[30]

Barn owl pellets are a thing of wonder, not least because they provide so much forensic evidence about their diet. Pellets are all undigested remains – the bones, feather and fur – of the barn owl's victims, which the bird has to regurgitate after a meal. As the barn owl tends to swallow its prey whole, picking apart a compact pellet can reveal information about the quantities and species of prey being consumed. Most pellets contain the remains of between three and six little creatures and studying their contents can say something important about how the barn owl's diet has changed over decades. Shifts in farming practices, for example, have resulted in a reduction in the number and diversity of prey animals for the barn owl – field voles, for example, don't seem to thrive on intensively farmed land. When you know that rough grassland can contain between 25 and 250 voles per hectare (100m^2), while a similar area of farmed landscape might contain as few as 15 voles,[31] it's easy to see why conservation groups are encouraging landowners to set aside areas of rough grassland. Even road verges have higher densities of field voles – at 25–45 per hectare – a feature that makes them both enticing and lethal for barn owls. Positive changes to farming practice also show themselves in pellet analysis. When the 'set-aside' scheme was introduced in the UK in 1988, which encouraged farmers to take strips of land out of agricultural production for wildlife and conservation, the number of wood mice appearing in the barn owl's diet showed a dramatic increase.

Barn owls aren't known for eating roadkill or other carrion. This is for a number of reasons; the first is that the barn owl detects its prey largely through sound and movement, qualities notably absent in a dead animal. Researchers also suspect that the barn owl's vision isn't fantastically good at discerning detail, particularly in the daytime, making it tricky for them to spot a squashed opportunity. That said, there have been at least two recordings of a barn owl eating roadkill in Britain, both of which may have been driven by starvation and bad weather. One was in East Lothian, Scotland, where an owl was found eating a pigeon that had been killed by a traffic collision (the barn owl was found to be severely underweight thanks to a harsh, snowy winter) and the other was a report of a barn owl attempting to eat a dead hedgehog, again in Scotland. The fact that these two isolated incidents were felt to be significant enough to report, and they occurred over thirty years apart, suggests that barn owl scavenging is highly unusual behaviour.[32]

HUNTING

Barn owls are undoubtedly masters of aerial stealth and have developed a number of hunting strategies to maximise their chances of a successful strike. The first technique is 'quartering', gliding slowly and silently just two or three metres above an area of open grassland. Here, the barn owl takes a methodical approach, flying carefully back and forth to make sure every square metre has been scanned for sound.

If the barn owl hears a noise from below, it will stop and hang silently in air, using its hearing and, to a lesser extent, its sight to lock on to the target. Once the barn owl has determined the exact position of the prey, it will position its body ready for the kill. In an instant, the barn owl plunges head-first towards the ground. As the bird drops, just moments before it hits the ground, the barn owl suddenly brings its face upward, swings its long legs forward and spreads its talons, ready for the moment of impact.

Recent research has also revealed that the barn owl keeps its legs bent until the last second, when it extends them as it drops on to its prey. It was thought that this action helped the owl cushion its landing, but the reverse seems to be true; the barn owl is using the last-minute straightening of its legs to add extra force, bringing a huge amount of power to the final strike – perhaps as much as the equivalent of a 12-ton truck squashing an adult[33] – often killing the prey in an instant. If the brute force of the landing doesn't finish off the unsuspecting creature, a squeeze from the barn owl's talons or a bite to the head with its hooked beak will dispatch the prey in seconds. Once the catch is dead, if the barn owl isn't returning straight to the nest, it sweeps its wings around the kill in a behaviour called 'mantling'. Like a vampire's cloak, the barn owl's wings can shield its quarry from greedy spectators and allow it to enjoy its meal in peace. If the barn owl misses its prey on a first attempt, it will often hop or skip along the ground, following its victim and readying itself for a second chance. This kind of hunting strategy is called 'leap and strike', a technique perfected for hunting from a standing start. As the bird leaps up from the floor, it gives only a few flaps of its wings to get it above its target, before diving head first back down, ready to strike.[34]

In the colder months, when energy is being used up by the effort just to keep warm, the barn owl may also employ a different hunting technique. Constantly quartering back and forth uses lots of energy, so the barn owl will often utilise 'perch and wait' hunting. It will find a vantage point such as a branch or fence post, preferably sheltered, and attempt to find prey by watching, scanning the ground and biding its time. This technique can take the barn owl much longer to locate a prey item but what the bird loses in minutes and hours it makes up for in lack of energy expended.

Did you know?

Barn owls are also known to occasionally 'bush beat', an ingenious technique where the barn owl flies close to a hedge or tree with small birds roosting inside, and wafts air into the branches with its beating wings. This is thought to startle the birds out from under cover, hopefully leaving the barn owl one or two sleepy stragglers to pounce on.

Chapter Four

LOVE

Summer has burst through into its final month.
August is only a few days old but the owlets
are already racing ahead, eager to reach the biggest
milestone yet – their inaugural flight.
Like a team of trainee flying aces, the two-month-old
chicks have been studiously practising their
wing-flapping exercises for the past fortnight
and are keen to test their mettle.

They almost look the part. Now slimmer and
taller than their six-week selves, from a distance
they could be mistaken for adult barn owls.
On closer inspection, however, there's still plenty
of fluff left to shed. The oldest owlet is nearly there
– his wings are looking sleek and flight-worthy, but
clumps of baby down persist all over his body.
He's a barn owl after a hot spin in a tumble dryer –
with every excitable wing flap, tiny fuffs of white
fluff waft into the air like a burst pillow.

It'll take a week or so to get the hang of things but, like
any good pilot, it's all about putting in the flying hours.
For now, he'll spend his days 'hop-flying' –
a hybrid of running, jumping and short, earnest flaps
around the barn. For just a few glorious moments
he's airborne, feet barely leaving the ground, but it's
enough to get a sense of what's to come. He's also
making good progress with his hunting, perfecting
the art of pouncing on unsuspecting feathers and bits
of straw as they drift with a late summer breeze.

The family is close-knit; the parents have been
preening each other for months but the siblings now
regularly nibble and massage each other's heads, backs
and necks with their beaks, a gesture that's thought
to bond the owlets and soothe tensions. The youngest
chicks often do the lion's share, obsequiously preening
their older siblings, but their attentiveness reaps
rewards. In return for every good scratch, an older
sibling is more likely to share its food, a win-win
transaction that ensures everyone is content.

Back on the stone ledge, the eldest takes his longest hop flight yet. It's good progress but, for all the chicks, this is perhaps one of their most perilous moments. Learning to fly is fraught with risk. In the barn, the hay bales provide plenty of soft landing, but for owlets elsewhere, nesting in tree stumps, overconfidence can lead to disaster. Even if they survive a bad crash landing, the owlet still has to avoid being trampled, rain-soaked or snatched as it works out how to get back home, with mother powerless to help. Luckily, owlets are good students and in just a few days they'll have graduated from flight school and be ready to take to the skies. The next big challenge will be putting together everything they've learned so far and attempting to catch their first dinner...

❦

FINDING A MATE

For a bird so often associated with solitude, the barn owl's private life is actually one of nature's greatest love stories. Barn owls mate for life, remaining affectionate and faithful to each other year after year. After the breeding season is over, and the fledglings have all left the nest, some couples decide to stay together throughout the rest of the year, keeping each other company and roosting at the same site. Other barn owl pairs will amicably separate when owlet-rearing duties are over, and spend a few months apart, before finding each other again at the beginning of the following breeding season.

Most male parents, however, 'move out' of the nest when the chicks first hatch a month after being laid; like a doting father, the male barn owl will roost close by and constantly visit his family, bringing food and checking up on progress. The mother stays with the chicks, day and night, for the first three or four weeks, after which point she can leave the nest for brief periods of hunting. By the time they are six weeks old, although the youngsters will continue to be fed by one or both parents, mother and father usually roost elsewhere.

Did you know?
When fledglings leave the nest, they disperse and find their own new home ranges. In the UK, the average dispersal distance seems to be around 12km (7 miles), but in other parts of the world this distance can be much greater. One American study, over a period of nearly twenty years, recorded an average distance of around 100km (62 miles), but the longest flight taken exceeded a heroic 1,000km (620 miles).[35]

If the weather is mild and food is plentiful, barn owls can go on to produce a second brood later in the summer. Depending on the timing, these two nests of chicks may even overlap – with one nest full of nearly independent adolescents and a second, nearby, with tiny newborns. Studies suggest that an average of ninety to a hundred days pass between the first and second clutch arriving – so the earlier a family starts breeding, the better chance they have of raising two separate broods before the weather turns cold. And while some second broods will hatch after the first have flown the nest, feeding both families simultaneously must be like spinning plates, a non-stop, unrelenting search for prey.

In times when food supplies dip, or hunting is delayed by bad weather, it's not unknown for older owlets who can fly to raid the new nest for food and, unfortunately, sometimes even take a baby sibling from the second brood.[36] A reliable supply of small mammals is crucial to the success of multiple broods – in sunnier climates than the UK's, barn owls seem to produce second clutches more often. Studies in California showed that over half the barn owl couples recorded managed to raise a second brood, while in one particularly mouse-rich year in Zimbabwe, one pair raised an astonishing four families.[37]

Once a juvenile barn owl has left home in early autumn, the search for its own mate begins. Over winter, males and females may begin the courtship ritual but the weather can often interrupt proceedings, causing the relationship to stop-start-stop over a number of weeks. Many barn owls will be familiar with their home ranges, and already know their potential mates; however, a juvenile male, who is new to the process, will often have to engage in a 'song flight' to attract a willing female to a potential nesting site. Making more of a plaintive screech than a lilting love song, the young male's calls are a series of hoarse, repetitive two-second screams — as many as five hundred a night.

If his calls are successful, and a female comes to investigate, his second wooing strategy kicks in — a flying display. At this stage, it's by no means a sure thing — single females may visit a number of potential suitors before deciding who has impressed her the most. The male may fly in circles and short bursts around the nest, inviting her to take a look. Like a nervous, over-eager first dater, he may even show her around the nest site, as if to demonstrate what a fine egg-laying place it would make.

If the female barn owl decides she likes what she

sees, they'll start spending more time together over the next few weeks. Like a rom-com montage, they'll flit from joint flights to cheek-rubbing and mutual preening. All this heavy petting is a precursor to the next stage, where the male starts to bring endless gifts of small mammals for his intended. On the face of it, the presents are a bonding gesture, but they also serve a deeper purpose — to fatten up the female ready for mating and egg-laying. A month before the first egg will be laid, the male might bring just one or two creatures a day, but a week before they plan to start their brood, the daily gifts can reach an overwhelming ten or fifteen tiny animals in a single twenty-four-hour period.[38]

In fact, there seems to be an interesting relationship between the volume and quality of food brought to the nest by the male and the number of eggs the female will lay. At about twenty-five days before the female is due to lay, she'll still be popping in and out of the nest for the occasional bite to eat — one study estimated that, at this stage, the female barn owl is still spending around 20 per cent of her time away from the nesting site. As laying day looms closer, however, the female bird spends more and more time in the nesting site until, with about a week to go, she'll stay put and rely entirely on the food her mate can fetch home. One fascinating piece of research found that the female seems able to adjust how many eggs she will lay based on her assessment of how well her partner is providing for her. The clutch size seems to be determined a few days before laying, just at the point at which the male barn owl is showing how many small mammals he's capable of catching – the theory is that the female barn owl is using the male's food provisioning to estimate both his hunting skills and how plentiful the food supply is in his home range.[39]

Did you know?

Baby owlets have similar sleep patterns to human babies. Sleep in mammals consists of two phases – REM sleep, where our brains are in a state of semi-wakefulness, and deep sleep. No one really knows what the purpose of REM sleep is, but young mammals and barn owls seem to get lots of it and, as they get older, need less. Newborns, for example, spend about half their sleep time in REM but in adults it's more like 20 per cent. One theory is that REM sleep acts like a workout for the growing brain, helping it to form mature neural connections even when the body is asleep.

REPRODUCTION

If there was a prize for love-making, barn owls would definitely be in the running. A month before the female starts laying, a barn owl couple might copulate once a day. As the time for laying gets closer, however, the pace can increase to a frenzied once an hour. One study even recorded a pair mating an exhausting seventy times in one day.[40] Why barn owls have sex so often isn't fully understood – one thought is that such frequent copulation is designed to make sure the sperm of any other male who sneakily mates with the female would be diluted. Barn owls continue to mate frequently, however, right through the hatching and owlet-rearing phase – a sign, perhaps, that the act is as much about pair bonding as breeding.

To initiate sex, the male barn owl often brings the female a prey item, a wooing enticement that she keeps jealously grasped in her beak even mid-act. When the gift is presented to the female, she accepts it and then crouches into position, making it easier for the male barn owl to climb on top. It's not easy to balance on a feathered, wobbling barn owl, and so the male has to grab hold of the female's neck with his beak and, like a tightrope walker, open out his wings for balance. Luckily, he doesn't have to keep steady for long – a brief thirty seconds on average and it's all over. At least for the next few hours anyway.

DIVORCE

But even the best relationships can falter. According to a recent study, it was noticed that, in about a quarter of pairings, one of the barn owls will 'divorce' their companion and try to find a new mate. Why a bird that is usually monogamous would choose to leave a partner in whom it has invested time and energy is an interesting question. Researchers who studied the species in Switzerland over a period of twenty-five years concluded that although barn owls are naturally faithful birds, they will 'divorce' if breeding isn't successful. An unusually low number of eggs, for example, or a brood of sickly chicks may be enough to convince one of the pair to cut their losses and find a new mate mid-season or, if it's too late in the breeding cycle, wait until the following year. Swapping partners is a risky strategy, however, as nestling survival increases with every year a pair are faithful to each other.

Barn owls aren't always models for fidelity either. A number of cases have been recorded of a male barn owl managing to simultaneously sire and raise two different families by two different females. In most cases the female barn owls were sufficiently far enough away from each other not to know the 'other woman' existed, but the effort needed to find food for two hungry broods must have been extraordinary.[41] In a handful of instances, polygamous males have been known to have female partners nest close together, some even sitting side-by-side companionably in the same nest.

Female barn owls, meanwhile, occasionally abandon their first broods, leaving the male partner in sole charge, to set up a second brood with a different mate. She doesn't, however, always stay with the new male, who is often younger and less experienced.[42] One theory is that the female treats the second brood as a kind of safety net – an extra chance to increase her overall reproductive success for the year.

Incestuous relationships are also uncommon but not unknown. In two studies, between 0.6 per cent and 1.2 per cent of barn owl couples were closely related, a reassuringly low figure as breeding between family members often results in genetic disorders.[43] New fledglings leave their nest and home range, and travel some distance, to avoid this very problem, although there may also be some other mechanism, such as familial recognition, that discourages relatives from inbreeding.

Did you know?

There's an unusual connection between owls, C. S. Lewis and Valentine's Day. The collective noun for all owls, including the barn owl, is a 'parliament'. The name appears in the C. S. Lewis classic The Chronicles of Narnia, which described a council of wise owls who would meet at night to discuss Narnia's affairs. Lewis, however, borrowed the term from Chaucer's fourteenth-century poem Parliament of Fowls, which talked about a group of birds who would gather in spring on 'seynt valentynes day' to pick their mate for the forthcoming year.

Chapter Five

CHALLENGES

It's mid-August, harvest time.
For thousands of years, country folk wondered
how it was that so many mice, and other rodents,
seemed to surface from nowhere at this time
of year and, as Pliny complained, 'devour whole
fields of corne'. Medieval writers had a crackpot
theory: mice sprang from drops of water. The
'generation and procreation of Mice', wrote naturalist
Edward Topsell in 1607, 'is not only by copulation,
but also nature worketh wonderfully in engendering
them from earth and small showers of rain.'

Our small owlet, now grown up, could be forgiven
for thinking this too. Yesterday evening,
a brief summer storm seemed to bring the mice
out in their droves. When the rain stopped,
the young barn owl began to hunt, honing the skills
he'd been practising over the past two weeks.
From his initial, uncoordinated flights – full of crash

landings and mistimings – the owlet has now
taken dozens of short journeys outside, getting braver
and better by the day. All those preparatory jumps
and dives came in handy too. Tentative leaps
from the ground on to beetles, bugs, and anything else
that rustled in the long grass quickly graduated
to live prey. And just in time too – for some time
now his parents have been slowly reducing
his meals and, in the next week or so, will cut
off his food supply completely.

As for the mice, they're keeping their heads down.
Soon the rest of the owlets will be out hunting
too, and it'll be a race to see how quickly
they can perfect the art before the five brothers
and sisters go their separate ways. The mice are
probably hoping for a rainy few weeks ahead.
Not only will it spoil the barn owls' plans
but research suggests that warm, drizzly nights
encourage mice to make an appearance

because the raindrops mask the rodents'
scurrying sounds and scents.[44] *Turns out that,*
just as the medieval writers believed,
summer showers might just magically make
the mice appear after all...

ENEMIES

The barn owl is wise to inhabit the night. Under the cover of darkness, they can fly and eat without being disturbed. But many barn owls don't stick to the curfew and head out at dusk, dawn and even during the day – a risky strategy when there are foes about.

There are a number of reasons a barn owl might get attacked. Groups of smaller birds are known to mob the barn owl if they're protecting their young – aerial battles can often take place between crows, ravens, rooks, gulls and other doughty day birds, who will give chase until the barn owl flies off. Other predatory birds have been known to perform hit-and-runs on the barn owl in an attempt to steal their food – in the UK, it's not uncommon to see common kestrels grabbing prey from a barn owl mid-air.

And although barn owls are, in many ways, at the top of the food chain, there are a handful of creatures who present a threat. Across Europe, species known to eat the barn owl include Eurasian eagle owls, buzzards and northern goshawks. In the US, great horned owls have been known to attack barn owls, but nest-raiding mammals such as racoons also present a danger. In the UK, common buzzards, peregrine falcons and sparrowhawks have been known to dispatch barn owls but, in turn, barn owls have been recorded predating on another native species, the 'little owl', on at least two occasions.[45]

Barn owls and tawny owls occasionally come into conflict. Tawny owls are ferociously protective of their territory and may become aggressive if their paths collide with other predatory birds. Mother tawny owls are notoriously fierce when it comes to defending their nests and will often make a pre-emptive strike if feeling threatened – pioneering wildlife photographer Eric Hosking famously lost his left eye when a tawny owl attacked his face, talons outstretched. Tawny owls have also been filmed flying at full speed at barn owls, knocking them off perches and out of nest boxes and violently evicting them from favourite nesting places. Tawny owls also tend to start nesting earlier in the season and have been known to take up residence in a barn owl nest while both parents are at their winter roosting sites. As much as the barn owl might want to defend its nest, it knows when it's beaten – although barn and tawny owls are a similar height, the tawny is a much stronger, beefier bird, weighing nearly one-and-a-half times as much.

The barn owl will, however, courageously defend its nest and owlets. Spats can occur between barn owls and kestrels or tawny owls, or when mammals such as cats, stoats and other predators approach. The barn owl's first line of defence is a series of short hisses and tongue-clicks, often accompanied by lowering of its head and arching the wings. If the danger persists, the barn owl might sway its body and attempt to strike out with its talons. If the attack comes from above, the barn owl may even lie on its back, helping it to kick out with its legs. Even Pliny the Elder, writing in the first century AD, noted this tactic in young owls. 'The owlet', he wrote, 'shows considerable shrewdness in its engagements with other birds; for when surrounded by too great a number, it throws itself on its back, and so, resisting with its feet, and rolling up its body into a mass, defends itself with the beak and talons.'[46]

Did you know?
Barn owls aren't aggressive birds, but they do have a number of defensive strategies if they come under attack. One of the most surprising is 'playing dead'. When a barn owl is handled, it may appear to go rigid and lifeless, stiff as a lollipop. Some experienced handlers can even induce this state by laying the barn owl gently on its back.

THREATS

For all the tawny owls' bullying, barn owls face much graver dangers from humankind. The knowledge that, in captivity, barn owls can live for two decades but, out in the wild, less than 40 per cent survive their first year begs the question: 'What's going wrong?' Nature, red in tooth and claw, is undoubtedly tough but human factors seem to be playing a large part in barn owl mortality. From flying into overhead electric cables to drowning in cattle troughs, the barn owl has to dodge a wide array of obstacles in the countryside.

Some of the threats have improved in recent years – the 1981 Wildlife and Countryside Act, which gave protection to native wild bird species and their habitats, stopped people being able to deliberately injure or kill barn owls, or damage their nests or eggs. Organochlorine pesticides such as aldrin and dieldrin, which were implicated in barn owl deaths, were also thankfully banned across the UK, US and EU by the early 1980s. Unfortunately, the barn owl still faces some major man-made challenges, with road accidents, rodenticides and habitat loss top of the list.

ROAD ACCIDENTS

According to The Barn Owl Trust, road accidents are now responsible for more barn owl deaths than any other single cause, with alarming estimates of between three and five thousand barn owls killed by traffic collisions every year in Britain alone.[47] Studies over time have revealed that, as numbers of cars and roads increase, barn owl deaths have also accelerated – in the 1950s, about 15 per cent of all recorded barn owl deaths were road casualties. Over the following decades, the figures raced depressingly upwards – 30 per cent in the late 1960s, 40 per cent in the 1970s, and reaching around 50 per cent on today's roads.

There are a number of factors at play: not only has the volume and speed of vehicles increased over this time but the type of road has also changed. Faster roads – such as motorways and dual carriageways – are exponentially more lethal for barn owls than minor roads; the density of traffic is not only greater on these kinds of roads but the speeds are also quicker, making it more difficult for either the driver or the barn owl to avoid the other. To demonstrate the point, although only one in fifty of Britain's roads are motorways or dual carriageways, they account for over 90 per cent of barn owl casualties.[48]

There are some unexpected problems too – high-sided lorries are particularly tricky for barn owls, who get sucked into the slipstream, while fast arterial roads also tend not to be flanked by hedges or trees that encourage the barn owl to fly higher over the road. New roads often cut into existing countryside or leave only road verges for barn owls to hunt on, forcing them to fly perilously close to traffic. Verges are often the last vestige of wilderness for many native species – in Britain, roadsides have been recorded as being valuable breeding habitat for at least twenty species of small mammals, forty species of birds, six species of reptiles and the same number of amphibians.[49] It's perhaps no surprise that, given a lack of such species-rich environments elsewhere, barn owls would choose to hunt there.

CHEMICALS

Factors often combine in lethal ways. Poisons used to kill rodents have ended up inadvertently harming barn owls. One of the main ways that rodenticides work is by stopping their blood from clotting. Anticoagulant poisons are eaten by the rat or mouse, which then causes internal bleeding and the animal dies. While many rodenticides are now labelled for 'indoor use only' or specify that the bait has to be covered if placed outdoors, it can take the rodent up to two weeks to die, leaving plenty of time for it to scuttle outside, only to be eaten by a barn owl. Or, in some instances, 'indoor use' is misinterpreted as safe for use in barns and other open farm buildings, where rodents and barn owls can freely mix.

If eating between one and five contaminated rodents is enough to kill a barn owl, it wouldn't take long for the bird to find enough poisoned prey in a short period of time. And even if it takes a few weeks or months to eat enough toxic prey, anticoagulant poisons stay in the body for a long period, lethally accumulating over time.

To add to the problem, conservationists also suspect that these toxic chemicals, even at very low levels, may be affecting the barn owls' physiology and ability to function properly. A 'drugged' owl is more likely to have traffic collisions and, if struck by a vehicle, is more likely to bleed to death. It's also thought that these sub-lethal doses may impair the barn owl's ability to hunt and forage, leaving many prone to starvation. What's truly staggering is the numbers of birds who have ingested some kind of anticoagulant rodenticide, even if it hasn't been the primary cause of their mortality: a recent study found that nearly nine out of every ten barn owls found dead in Britain from any cause had traces of anticoagulant rat poison in their systems.[50]

HABITAT LOSS

Farming has had to work hard to meet the demands of a growing population who want cheap food. Intensive agriculture tries to get the most productivity out of a unit of land, whether that's by increasing the use of fertiliser and pesticides, having higher densities of animals grazing on a plot of land, or planting high-yield crops. The mechanisation of farming and reducing fallow or waste land has also helped to increase farming's output and take away much of the drudgery. There's a fine balance, however, between squeezing as much as we can from the land and long-term sustainability, not only of the soil but also all the other creatures who rely on the countryside.

Barn owls are not woodland creatures, nor have they readily adapted to urban life. They are birds of the open countryside and, for a long time, have managed to co-exist with farmers. They don't necessarily need a perfect wilderness to thrive. There are plenty of areas in a traditional mixed farming landscape that can support barn owls – from wide field margins to winter stubble, hedgerows to watercourse banks. Rough grassland that is lightly grazed is also an ideal habitat – packed to the brim with tiny voles, mice and shrews. The problems come when these slightly scruffier, 'less productive' areas come under threat, whether it's from changes in agricultural practice and policy or new housing and transport developments. Agriculture is a powerful force behind changes in land use – an increasing number of people are realising it's important to understand that farming policy and biodiversity are interconnected, and that sustainable agriculture can actively benefit not only wildlife, but the rural community as custodians of the landscape. In the last chapter, we'll see how both farmers and landowners are making changes that are bringing barn owls back on to their land.

Habitat loss isn't just about fields and hedgerows, however. Like any human landscape, the farmed environment is ever changing. It's impossible to preserve the countryside in aspic, and nor should we. One of the issues for barn owls, however, has been their loss of nesting sites – in particular, the removal of traditional farm buildings and the conversion of barns to domestic dwellings. Many of these agricultural buildings no longer serve their original purpose and no good is served by letting them fall into such disrepair that neither humans nor barn owls can make use of them. However, the renovation or removal of such buildings needs to take into account the welfare of the many species that rely on them – whether it's bats, solitary bees or barn owls. Building for biodiversity has to be part of the future of planning. In the final chapter, we'll see how planners, builders and homeowners can make small changes, such as erecting barn owl nest boxes, to help protected species continue to live and breed in their traditional home ranges.

Chapter Six

HELP

It's the first week of September, the month of
reckoning. For many cultures, this is the moment
when all the year's hard work comes to fruition.
For the Anglo-Saxons, September was Halegmonaþ,
the 'holy month', a time for celebrations and sacrifices.
The gods were to be rewarded for their bounty –
all the crops, livestock and new life that flourished
over the past few months and helped ensure the
group's survival until the following year.

In the barn, the barn owls are experiencing their
own reckoning of sorts. The breeding season
has come to an end and all five owlets are ready to
leave. It's been fourteen weeks of almost non-stop
parental care – the hundreds of night-flights
and food excursions have taken their toll on both
parents. June and July were the hardest months for
the father – the endless food-gathering used up
enormous amounts of energy and his weight dipped.
Unlike the female, who moulted her feathers when

she was calmly sitting on her eggs, the exhausted
male has waited until now to renew his frayed feathers.
Thankfully, their heroic efforts have paid off.
All five chicks have made it to adulthood,
a miraculous feat by anyone's standards.

All along the way, there have been dangers.
Eggs can fail to hatch, and nestlings frequently
don't make it to this point – just three out of five
chicks surviving to the fledgling stage is considered a
success. From here on, however, family life ceases.
All the fledgling barn owls must move away and find
their own ranges – some will only go a few miles;
others may travel much further in search of a place
to call home. It's anyone's guess where they'll go.
Some of the siblings may even roost in the same
place, or reassuringly close by, for a while.
Mother and father might carry on roosting
together or decide to go it alone for the next few
months before reuniting later down the line.

There will not, however, be any warm family reunions. Young barn owls need to get away from the natal nest and find a patch of their own countryside that can provide plenty of food and, hopefully, a new partner come early spring. The next few months will be make or break for our inexperienced owl – there are so many obstacles in his way, especially now summer is slipping into autumn. If the fledglings bump into mother or father from now on, they'll probably get short shrift – young owls are often ignored by their parents. It's tough love but necessary – in only six months or so, and with a fair wind behind him, our new owl will be starting a family of his very own...

❧

WHERE TO SEE BARN OWLS

In the UK, barn owls are widely distributed, apart from snow-prone upland areas and the most northerly regions. In Ireland, the population is sadly declining, and is mainly concentrated in the middle and south-west. The barn owl's preferred habitat is lowland farmland, so head out into the open countryside if you want to catch a glimpse. Their absolute favourite type of hunting ground is rough grassland, but arable fields, hedgerows, riverbanks, wide verges, railway embankments and woodland edges are also hotspots. East Anglia, Lincolnshire and East Yorkshire – with their large stretches of flat farmland – are traditionally rich in barn owls but, even though barn owls are not evenly distributed through the UK, almost every rural county has some. Barn owls may even set up home on rural fringes and large urban green open spaces. See Directory (pages 154–5) for a list of UK nature reserves known for their barn owls.

WHEN TO SEE BARN OWLS

For much of the year, barn owls are creatures of dusk and dawn, so head out either early in the morning or as the sun begins to set. Their numbers peak around August and September, when young barn owls have fledged and recently left the nest. Barn owls also hate rain and strong wind – you won't tend see them out in bad weather, but their activity will increase straight after, when they'll be at their hungriest. Barn owls also hunt in the day at two particular times of the year – one is during winter when night temperatures fall below 0°, which also pushes field voles out into the daytime – and the other is in summer if there's a brood to feed and the nights have been too rainy to hunt. The good news is that, once you've glimpsed one, you'll likely see it a few more times over the following days and weeks – barn owls hunt over the same area and often stick to a roughly similar routine. You may even work out which are their favourite posts and perches.

Nature groups and wildlife sanctuaries often organise

'owl prowls', guided walks led by a conservation expert who can lead you to the most likely locations where barn owls are active. You'll also learn how to distinguish the barn owl call from other native species.

If you can't get out and about, there are a number of 'live owl cams' that give you a fascinating glimpse into nest life (see Directory, page 153–4).

Getting close

Barn owls and humans have co-existed for centuries, but they wisely keep us at a distance. They're not skittish, however, so if you can keep quiet and still, you'll often be rewarded with a good few minutes of flying or perching before the barn owl moves on. The Wildlife Trust suggests that, if a barn owl is hunting nearby, you may be able to attract its attention by making a rodent-like squeaking noise by kissing the back of your hand. It may even come closer to investigate the source of the noise. Disturbing or in any other way harming barn owls is against the law.

HOW TO HELP BARN OWLS

When many of the problems facing the barn owl are related to the changing landscape, it is difficult to see how we can help. Some of the suggestions below are aimed at farmers, landowners and policymakers, but there are also things we can do on a small scale to protect this beautiful bird. In the Directory (pages 151–155) is a number of charities and organisations who are dedicated to protecting the barn owl and its environment – support them, volunteer, champion the barn owl. This book is intended to be a first step towards finding out more.

Creating habitat

In the UK, barn owls traditionally prefer permanent rough grassland, areas of long tussocky grass that aren't regularly mown or heavily grazed by animals. This is a very specific type of environment – where the grass has been allowed to grow long, collapse and die, and then new grass grows up through it. This creates something called a 'litter layer' – the matted dead grass that you see when you part the green grass with your hands – and forms a wonderful year-round cover for voles and other small mammals to tunnel their way through. Rough grassland also supports a whole ecosystem of other wildlife – from native flowers to butterflies, mammals to birds.

Barn owls tend to stick to the countryside so there's little point turning an urban backyard over to rough grassland. That said, if you do happen to have a large garden containing newly planted woodland, a fence line, a drainage ditch, a paddock, a steep bank, a field margin, or any other area of grassland that could be made barn-owl-friendly, it all adds to the bigger picture. As the countryside fragments, creating patches of rough grassland adds to the total sum of land available for barn owls to hunt over. These kinds of areas are most useful to the barn owl if they're in blocks or wide strips along field edges, hedgerows, riverbanks, edges of woodland or verges alongside quiet tracks (i.e. footpaths, bridleways, farm tracks). It's important to add, however, that rough grassland shouldn't be deliberately created within 1km (½ mile) of a busy road, as this puts the owls at a greater risk of traffic injury.

Creating rough grassland isn't the same as leaving an area to go wild – it'll need occasional management to stop it being overrun by brambles or scrub. The idea is that you leave the grass to grow as normal, without mowing or grazing, throughout spring and summer of year one. By late summer the grass will be so long it'll collapse and start to die, creating a matted, dead layer. Don't panic: next spring, in year two, the new grass will grow up through the old grass and become a thick cover for voles, mice and shrews. Later that summer or in the early autumn you can either top, brush-cut or mow the grass (watching out for hedgehogs and slow-worms) to a height of no less than about 10cm (4in), or allow cattle to lightly graze until winter (sheep tend to graze too close to the ground). Do this every alternate or third year. Ultimately, the aim is to create areas of thick, bouncy cover, not short tufts like a lawn or closely grazed pasture.

Not every space has the potential for areas of rough grassland, but barn owls can make the most of other habitats at different times of the year – fields of winter stubble can support large numbers of wood mice, who will gorge on the leftover grain during the hardest months, while recently cut hay meadows can provide a boost of exposed prey in late summer. While barn owls are not woodland birds, they can make use of newly planted areas of woodland. Research has shown that while the young trees are getting established in the first two to seven years, barn owls can make good use of the grassy spaces in between the saplings. Once the trees have grown, woodland edges and rides can still be a draw for barn owls. Native hedgerows with a grassy margin at their base can also be a rich source of prey, and they provide cover for lots of small mammals.

Nest boxes

Barn owls need plenty of prey, but they also need somewhere to raise their young. Unlike some other wild creatures, barn owls seem to take readily to nest boxes, especially when there are few other options available. Badly built or positioned nest boxes are, however, lethal for barn owls and so it's vital to get them right. The Barn Owl Trust are *the* people to consult about anything to do with nest boxes, land management, feeding barn owls and supporting barn owl conservation (see Directory, page 151). They also have free barn owl nest box plans, depending on where you need to put the nest box. In order of preference, the Trust recommends placing the nest box inside a building, followed by a tree nest box and finally on a pole – each position needs a slightly different design. Barn owl nest boxes also need to be cleaned out at the right time of the year (between November and January) and positioned within the landscape away from hazards and for maximum access to prey.

If you are renovating a rural building or creating a new one, there are plenty of ways to incorporate barn owl nesting sites within its construction. Barn conversions traditionally take away some of the last refuges for the barn owl, who may have occupied a home range for a number of years. Creating a new home not only mitigates the effects for one barn owl family but will also allow new barn owl pairs to stay in the area for the future. The Royal Institute of British Architects (architecture.com) has a brilliant guide called *Designing for Biodiversity: A technical guide for new and existing buildings*, which explains how you can provide permanent provision for barn owls, and a host of other wildlife, in the built environment. Get it right and the results can be dramatic – as we've already learned, up to three-quarters of the UK's barn owls probably now nest in man-made boxes.

Tree hollows

Barn owls nest in hollows, which only appear in old trees. Hollows can start for a number of reasons – lightning might strike the trunk or a branch may fall off, leaving an 'open wound' on the bark. Fungi, bacteria and insects get into the hole and then slowly, over a period of decades, make it large enough to attract the attention of other wildlife.

The older a tree becomes, the more useful it is to wildlife. Barn owls have utilised ancient trees since before the advent of farming, but the number of historic specimens is shrinking. Despite the fact that old trees, full of dead wood and scooped-out holes, can survive for hundreds of years, we're cutting them down at an alarming rate in the mistaken belief that a gnarly, veteran tree is a dangerous one.

The perfect tree for a barn owl is large, with a wide, elephantine trunk. The barn owl can't fly in dense woodland and so the ideal specimen will be isolated, alone on the edge of a field, for example, or tucked away in a hedgerow. Barn owls will also nest in trees on the edges of woodland.

Sometimes it is necessary to tackle a tree if it poses a risk to safety, but it's always important to explore other options before removing the entire specimen. Sometimes pruning or pollarding can remove the issue without sacrificing the tree and any wildlife that relies on it. A qualified arboriculturalist should be able to help you minimise the impact. In the UK, old trees often have Tree Preservation Orders (TPOs) on them, and you'll need permission from the local authority to do any work – a quick call to your planning office will tell you if there is a TPO on your tree. And if you think a tree is under threat from felling and want to protect it, you can ask the local authority to put an emergency protection order on it while they investigate whether it qualifies or not.

The law

If a barn owl is nesting in a tree hollow, damaging or destroying an active nest is against the law in the UK. Wild barn owls are covered by the 1981 Wildlife and Countryside Act, which forbids activities such as destroying a barn owl or its nest or eggs and catching wild barn owls to keep or sell. Cruelty to barn owls is also against the law and matters of welfare relating to both wild and captive barn owls fall within the legal framework of the Act. If you think a wild barn owl has been mistreated, poisoned or killed, it's a matter for the police and their Wildlife Liaison Officer. If you suspect a captive barn owl is being mistreated, the RSPCA should be your first port of call (see Directory, page 151).

Campaign

Barn owls need advocates. There are a number of dedicated charities and organisations across the world championing their cause and facing the issues head on. You can support individual campaigns – such as tackling the misuse of rodenticides – or get involved with wider conservation work and habitat recreation.

At a local level, you can put yourself forward for barn owl monitoring and recovery projects – almost every county has one – or volunteer for one of the many ornithological groups such as the RSPB, the Hawk and Owl Trust or the World Owl Trust. If you own or farm agricultural land and want to find out more about wildlife-friendly practices, there are plenty of enthusiastic groups willing to share their expertise, including the Soil Association, the Nature Friendly Farming Network and the Sustainable Food Trust. The Barn Owl Trust has specific advice for managing land for barn owls both on their website and in a detailed guide, *The Barn Owl Conservation Handbook*, which is especially useful for farmers and ecologists.

Many barn owl charities also sell purpose-built barn owl nest boxes and conservation guides, and offer useful advice about how to site nest boxes and manage land for barn owls. If you don't have space for your own nest box, you can always sponsor one through organisations such as the Hawk and Owl Trust or adopt a rescued barn owl through the work of The Barn Owl Trust.

The success of the barn owl is part of a wider picture. Many of the issues that affect barn owls also impact other wild creatures. Whether it's the loss of wild spaces, the encroachment of noise and light pollution, toxic chemicals and pesticides, shifts in seasons and temperatures, river damage, or changes to government funding that have a direct effect on an organisation's ability to monitor and protect the environment, we are at a pivotal moment. It's important to be optimistic about change – despair is a great demotivator – but that optimism has to come with action. Join a wildlife charity, lobby your local MP, educate your family, write an article, sign a petition, campaign, volunteer, spread the word or simply donate to a cause.

Some of the ways you can help may not be immediately obvious – eating more sustainably or growing your own, for example, helps take the pressure off intensive agriculture, which, in turn, helps the barn owl. Investing ethically in companies that have a positive environmental impact can force others to make changes.

Use politics to your advantage – find a party who makes a commitment to protecting wildlife and tackling the climate emergency and, at a local level, lobby your council or town board, who have a key role in protecting your patch of the environment. There's lots of advice online about how to have an open and productive dialogue with council officers and local councillors. Above all, find like-minded people who share your concerns – there's lots of us out there, eyes glued to the fields and hedgerows, hoping to see a flash of white.

DIRECTORY

UK CONSERVATION & ANIMAL PROTECTION

The Barn Owl Trust (UK)
www.barnowltrust.org.uk

British Trust for Ornithology
www.bto.org

Hawk and Owl Trust
www.hawkandowltrust.org

RSPB
www.rspb.org.uk

The Wildlife Trusts
www.wildlifetrusts.org

RSPCA
www.rspca.org.uk

BARN OWL CONSERVATION (WORLDWIDE)

Owl Research Institute (US)
www.owlresearchinstitute.org

The Peregrine Fund (US)
www.peregrinefund.org

Hungry Owl Project (US)
www.hungryowls.org

BirdLife International
www.birdlife.org

Barn Owl Protection (Netherlands)
www.kerkuil.com

Barn Owl Foundation (Hungary)
http://gyongybagoly.hu/index.php/en/

Barn Owl Project (Ireland)
www.thebarnowlproject.com/

Barn Owl Protection (Germany)
www.ag-eulenschutz.de

Birdlife Australia Raptor Group
www.birdlife.org.au/Locations/Barg

Society for the Preservation of Raptors (Australia)
www.raptor.org.au

WINGSPAN (New Zealand)
www.wingspan.co.nz

Galapagos Barn Owl
www.galapagosconservation.org.uk

African Raptor Centre (South Africa)
http://africanraptor.co.za

WILDLIFE-FRIENDLY FARMING

Nature Friendly Farming Network
www.nffn.org.uk

Sustainable Food Trust
www.sustainablefoodtrust.org

Wild Farm Alliance (US)
www.wildfarmalliance.org

BARN OWL NEST BOXES

Barn Owl Trust (UK)
www.barnowltrust.org.uk

Nestbox (UK)
www.nestbox.co.uk

NHBS (UK)
www.nhbs.com

Barn Owl Box Company (US)
www.barnowlbox.com

BARN OWL LIVE CAMS

Robert Fuller
www.robertefuller.com

Barn Owl Trust
www.barnowltrust.org.uk/Barn-Owl-Facts/Barn-Owl-Cams/

Somerset Wildlife Trust
www.somersetwildlife.org/swtbarnowls

WHERE TO SEE BARN OWLS

Wildlife Trust Nature Reserves including:
Anglesey – Cors Goch

Avon – Folly Farm

Cambridgeshire – The Great Fen, Grafham Water
and the Ouse Washes

Dorset – Lorton Meadows

Essex – Blue House Farm

Lancashire – Lunt Meadows

Lincolnshire – Willow Tree Fen, Gibraltar Point
and Vine House Farm

London – Frays Farm Meadows

Norfolk – Hickling Broad

Somerset – Westhay Moor

Suffolk – Hen Reedbeds and Snape Marshes

Wiltshire – Blakehill Farm

National Trust sites including:
Bristol – Tyntesfield

Buckinghamshire – Stowe

Cardigan – Penbryn Beach

Cornwall – Penrose

County Down – Mount Stewart

Gloucestershire – Sherborne Park

Herefordshire – Brockhampton Estate

Kent – Sissinghurst Castle

Norfolk – Blickling Estate

Somerset – Holnicote

Suffolk – Ickworth and Orford Ness

Surrey – Hatchlands Park

Warwickshire – Charlecote Park

RSPB Reserves including:

Cambridgeshire – Fowlmere Nature Reserve,
Nene Washes and Ouse Fen

Cumbria – Geltsdale

Kent – Capel Fleet

Norfolk – Rockland Marshes and Strumpshaw Fen

Suffolk – Boyton and Hollesley Marshes and Havergate Island

Warwickshire – Middleton Lakes

West Sussex – Pulborough Brooks

Yorkshire – Bempton Cliffs, Blacktoft Sands,
Dearne Valley Old Moor and Wheldrake Ings

NOTES

1 F. Willughby, FRS, *The Second Book of The Ornithology of Francis Willughby*, enlarged by John Ray, FRS (London, 1678), Sect. II. Of Nocturnal Rapacious Birds, Chapter II, Part III: The common Barn-Owl, or White-Owl, or Church-Owl.

2 W. E. Tate, *The Parish Chest: A Study of the Records of Parochial Administration in England* (Cambridge University Press, 1969), p. 106.

3 E. and M. A. Radford, *Encyclopaedia of Superstitions* (London: Rider and Company, 1947), p. 185.

4 Barn Owl Census, 1932, *Nature* 129, 790 (1932), https://doi.org/10.1038/129790d0

5 Map of barn owl population density in the United States: www.barnowlbox.com/barn-owls-by-state/

6 A. Roulin, *Barn Owls: Evolution and Ecology* (Cambridge University Press, 2020), p. 10.

7 www.birdguides.com/articles/first-dark-breasted-barn-owl-to-breed-in-britain/

8 V. Uva et al., 'Comprehensive molecular phylogeny of barn owls and relatives (Family: *Tytonidae*), and their six major Pleistocene radiations', *Molecular Phylogenetics and Evolution*, 125, 2018, pp. 127–37, https://doi.org/10.1016/j.ympev.2018.03.013

9 A. P. Machado et al., 'Unexpected post-glacial colonisation route explains the white colour of barn owls (*Tyto alba*) from the British Isles. *Molecular Ecology*, October 2021, https://doi.org/10.1111/mec.16250

10 A. Roulin et al., 'Female plumage spottiness signals parasite resistance in the barn owl (*Tyto alba*)', *Behavioral Ecology*, 12(1), January 2001, pp. 103–10, https://doi.org/10.1093/oxfordjournals.beheco.a000371

11 D. Ramsden et al., Barn Owl Trust, *Barn Owl Conservation Handbook* (Pelagic Publishing, 2012), p. 185.

12 www.owlresearchinstitute.org/owls-1

13 E. I. Knudsen, 'The Hearing of the Barn Owl', *Scientific American*, December 1981.

14 www.barnowl.co.uk/upload/docs/593/hearing_capabilities.pdf

15 L. Hausmann et al., 'Why are barn owls a model system for sound localization?', *Journal of Experimental Biology*, 213(14), 2010: pp. 2355–6, doi: 10.1242/jeb.034231

16 J. Tate Mason et al., 'Anthropogenic noise impairs owl hunting behavior', *Biological Conservation*, 199, 2016, pp. 29–32, doi.org/10.1016/j.biocon.2016.04.009

17 B. Krumm et al., 'Barn owls have ageless ears', *Proc. R. Soc. B*, 284(1863), 2017, http://doi.org/10.1098/rspb.2017.1584

18 Roulin, *Barn Owls: Evolution and Ecology*, p. 106.

19 K. LePiane and C. J. Clark, 'Evidence that the Dorsal Velvet of Barn Owl Wing Feathers Decreases Rubbing Sounds during Flapping Flight', *Integrative and Comparative Biology*, 60(5), November 2020, pp. 1068–79, https://doi.org/10.1093/icb/icaa045

20 I. Zuberogoitia et al., 'Moult in Birds of Prey: A Review of Current Knowledge and Future Challenges for Research', *Ardeola*, 65(2), 1 July 2018, pp. 183–207.

21 Roulin, *Barn Owls: Evolution and Ecology*, p. 113.

22 L. M. San-Jose et al., 'Differential fitness effects of moonlight on plumage colour morphs in barn owls', *Nature, Ecology & Evolution*, 3, 2019, pp. 1331–40, https://doi.org/10.1038/s41559-019-0967-2

23 M. Fux and D. Eilam, 'How barn owls (*Tyto alba*) visually follow moving voles (*Microtus socialis*) before attacking them', *Physiology & Behavior*, 98, 2009, pp. 359–66.

24 I. A. Taylor, 'How Owls Select Their Prey: A Study of barn owls *Tyto alba* and Their Small Mammal Prey', *Ardea* 97(4), pp. 635–44, 1 December 2009, https://doi.org/10.5253/078.097.0433

25 D. E. Glue, 'Prey taken by the barn owl in England and Wales', *Bird Study*, 14(3), 1967, pp. 169–83, doi: 10.1080/00063656709476160

26 R. S. Sommer et al., 'Bat predation by the barn owl *Tyto alba* in a hibernation site of bats', *Folia Zoologica* – Praha 58(1), 2009, pp. 98–103.

27 D. Chandler, *Barn Owl* (London: New Holland Publishers, 2011), p. 64.

28 R. Ille, 'Preference of Prey Size and Profitability in Barn Owls *Tyto alba guttata*', *Behaviour*, 116(3/4), 1991, pp. 180–89, www.jstor.org/stable/4534917, retrieved 18 March 2021.

29 M. Johnson and D. George, 'Estimating the Number of Rodents Removed by Barn Owls Nesting in Boxes on Winegrape Vineyards', Proceedings, 29th Vertebrate Pest Conference (D. M. Woods, Ed.), Paper No. 17. Published 28 August 2020.

https://wildlife.humboldt.edu/sites/default/files/johnson/pdf/
johnson_stgeorge_2020.pdf

30 D. E. Glue, 'Food of the Barn Owl in Britain and Ireland', *Bird Study*, 21(3), 1974, pp. 200–210, doi: 10.1080/00063657409476419

31 Ramsden et al., *Barn Owl Conservation Handbook*, p. 40.

32 S. Welch, 'A possible instance of a Barn Owl scavenging in severe weather', *Scottish Birds*, 32(4), 2012, pp. 300–1 and Dunsire, C. and Dunsire, R., 'Barn owl on dead hedgehog', *Scottish Birds*, 10(2), 1978, p. 56.

33 BBC Two, *Natural World*, Episode 1: Super Powered Owls (8 March 2015).

34 J. R. Usherwood et al., 'Leap and strike kinetics of an acoustically "hunting" barn owl (*Tyto alba*)', *Journal of Experimental Biology*, 217(17), 2014, pp. 3002–5, doi: 10.1242/jeb.107169

35 C. D. Marti, 'Natal and Breeding Dispersal in Barn Owls', *The Journal of Raptor Research*, 33(3), 1999, pp. 181–89, The Raptor Research Foundation, Inc.

36 R. Fuller, 'Barn Owl Chick Eats its Sibling | Stories from a Barn Owl Camera', www.youtube.com/watch?v=8HmTmcWW540&t=0s

37 Chandler, *Barn Owl*, pp. 64, 101–2.

38 Ramsden et al., *Barn Owl Conservation Handbook*, p. 62.

39 J. M. Durant et al., 'Behavioural and body mass changes before egg laying in the Barn Owl: Cues for clutch size determination?', *Journal of Ornithology*, 151(1), 2010, pp. 11–17, 10.1007/s10336-009-0415-1

40 Roulin, *Barn Owls: Evolution and Ecology*, p. 130.

41 Ibid., p. 135.

42 I. Henry et al., 'Multiple Paternity in Polyandrous Barn Owls (*Tyto alba*)', PLoS ONE 8(11): e80112. (2013), https://doi.org/10.1371/journal.pone.0080112

43 Ibid., p. 137.

44 A. Wróbel and M. Bogdziewicz, 'It is raining mice and voles: which weather conditions influence the activity of *Apodemus flavicollis* and *Myodes glareolus*?', *European Journal of Wildlife Research*, 61, 2015, pp. 475–8, https://doi.org/10.1007/s10344-014-0892-2

45 H. Mikkola, 'Owls killing and killed by other owls and raptors in Europe', *British Birds*, 69, 1976, https://britishbirds.co.uk/wp-content/uploads/article_files/V69/V69_N04/V69_N04_P144_154_A030.pdf

46 Pliny the Elder, *The Natural History*, John Bostock et al. (eds) (London: Taylor and Francis, 1855), chapter 19: The Owlet.

47 Ramsden et al., *Barn Owl Conservation Handbook*, p. 271.

48 www.barnowltrust.org.uk/hazards-solutions/barn-owls-major-roads/

49 F. Slater, 'Wildlife road casualties', http://programmeofficers.co.uk/Preston/CoreDocuments/LCC274.pdf

50 Walker et al. (2010), quoted in Ramsden et al., *Barn Owl Conservation Handbook*, p. 259.